BIBLE-CLASS BOATS

Janet and Bridget Cusack

This book is dedicated to our parents, Fred and Vera Cusack,
much of whose courting took place on trips with the Belmont Boating Club.

Belmont Men's Boating Club
Afloat in 1921 and ashore on a picnic at Notter bridge in 1919 with
Fred Cusack and Vera Wayment on the left in the front row.

This version of the book is virtually as originally published, presenting the work of Janet and Bridget Cusack.
There are now additional pages at the back providing information about the publisher, Arthur L Clamp.

The republishing project is being managed by Arthur's grandson, Steven Gibson. We aim to find all the research
that he was involved in publishing, preserving it for the next generation as part of 'The Clamp Collection'.

INTRODUCTION

Between 1900 and 1939 many churches and chapels in Plymouth, Devonport and Stonehouse sponsored rowing clubs for their young people. In the Sound and the Tamar the three towns enjoyed an ideal cruising ground which could probably not be equalled in Britain, and the presence of the Royal Naval Dockyard meant that second-hand boat prices, with some discreet 'rabbiting' added, made the purchase and fitting out of club vessels possible, while the many young men in apprenticeship in the Dockyard had skills which made maintenance costs of club boats minimal.

Sixty boating clubs have been identified so far. Twenty-eight were attached to Nonconformist churches, twenty of which were Wesleyan, Methodist or Primitive Methodist, while seven were Baptist and one Congregational (later United Reformed). Seventeen Anglican churches had boats, and the Roman Catholics had three, two of which were owned by individual churches, and the third by the Catholic Young Men's Club. Boats were also owned by Y.M.C.A. groups in Devonport and St. Budeaux. In addition nine organisations without any religious affiliation owned boats. For instance, a club, sponsored by the landlord, was based on the Royal Albert Bridge Inn and called *Brown Hilda* after the landlord's daughter, while another inn, in Pembroke Street, sponsored a gig, and club boats were also owned by the Plymouth Police, the Naval Stores Department and the Sutton Harbour Labour Party.

The boating clubs are still remembered with affection and pleasant nostalgia by former members, who are a valuable but, alas, diminishing source of information about the clubs they so enjoyed and recall so vividly. We ourselves grew up to many stories of the trips made by our parents in the Belmont boat, and we are most grateful to the generosity of those many other Plymothians and Devonport people who have been willing to share their memories of sunlit summer days on the Tamar, Plym and Sound in the years before the 1939-45 War.

This book has been written mainly from oral information, written descriptions and photograph albums shared with us by these former boating club members and their frequent guests. There are a very few documents which record club activities: some club fixture lists for rowing excursions have been cherished; the membership lists 1901-1939 of the St. George's Methodist Boating Club survive; some boating activities are recorded in the Devonport Y.M.C.A. magazines between 1909 and 1923. There is a minute book from the St. Budeaux Baptist Boating Club for the years between 1919 and 1922. Club activities are covered in a very few private documents, such as the private log of John Watson, describing his rowing in the Dockyard Church Boating Club between 1922 and 1926. News of church boating clubs rarely got into the local newspapers.

Historians, local as well as national, have virtually never turned their attention to these clubs which meant so much to so many local young people, and which were essentially the product of the circumstances of place and time in Plymouth, Devonport and Stonehouse in the early decades of the twentieth century.

Since our information is based on the words and photographs of senior citizens who have been kind enough to tell us about their boating excursions, it has not always been possible to date pictures and incidents closer than within five or six years.

We hope that readers will enjoy this book as much as we enjoyed the research, and that the stories and pictures that follow will help explain why, looking back to those golden days, one lady summed it all up by saying, 'You went to the boat and went up the River. It was lovely. You couldn't have done better if King George was your uncle'.

Janet and Bridget Cusack
10 Ranscombe Close
Brixham
South Devon TQ5 9UR

March 2000

St. Levan's Wesleyan Boating Club, Whit Monday 1929

St. George's Road Methodist Club, probably at Cawsand

THE BOATS

The young people of Plymouth and Devonport were fortunate in that there was a local supply of good cheap rowing boats. Naval cutters, gigs and whalers, surplus to service requirements, could be purchased from the Royal Naval Dockyard Boat Camber for a few pounds. The most popular boat among the clubs between 1919 and 1939 was a thirty-foot six-oar gig, as used by Stoke Damerel, St. Michael's, St. Bartholomew's and St. Stephen's churches, St. George's and Wycliffe chapels, and the Devonport Y.M.C.A. The boat used by the St. John's Church Club, Devonport, was an ex-seiner, while the Dockyard Church in the 1920s had a six-oared gig and a five-oared whaler. In 1919 St. Budeaux Baptist Men's Club used a whaler.

Club boating was an inexpensive hobby. The normal cost of a 'bare' boat purchased from the Dockyard boat Camber between the wars was £5, and when the St. Budeaux Baptists considered the purchase of a boat in 1919 the cost was estimated at £5 for the boat and £1 for twelve oars. However, many members of boating clubs worked in the Dockyard, or had friends in the Boat Camber, and there are numerous stories of how the purchase costs of boats and equipment could be reduced. For example: 'Ours was bought as a damaged boat from [a naval ship]. A shipwright was a club member, he saw to it that there was a small hole in the boat so that she was sold off as damaged, and then repaired it. She was a very good boat'. Also : 'We had friends in the yard who told them to go for Lot no 6, and when they paid their £5 for it, and took it away, they found that although boats were officially sold 'bare', some kind soul had added rowlocks, oars, spars and sails'. Other clubs with fathers or friends in Naval Signals had no problems in obtaining fabric for cushions and flags.

A very few boats passed from one club to another. When the Belmont Men's Club was revived in 1930 they bought a boat from St. Budeaux Baptist Club for £5. This was an 8-oar gig, formerly used by the captain of H.M.S. *Impregnable*.

Rowing Boat of St. George's Methodist Club, Stoke
The original 30-ft boat was purchased in 1901, and sat out the 1914-18 war in a field at Torpoint, 'all the oars were still there when it was collected at the end of the War. People were honest then'. The boat was replaced about 1928.

Most boats were rowed, but some clubs could sail. St. Bartholomew's gig in 1936 had a drop keel and a mainsail, although on most excursions it was rowed. St .George's Methodist Club second gig, shown below, had mast and sail.

St. George's Methodist Club Sailing Gig
This 36-foot carvel boat was built for the Naval Cadet's Club by the Plym Yachting Company, and passed by the Cadets into the Boat Camber, where it was spotted by the St. George's Club President who worked in the Stores.

A very few clubs used motor boats. St. Budeaux Baptist Senior Boat Club had an engined boat from the early 1930s. This was a 30-foot ex-Admiralty gig converted by members to carry an engine, The first power unit used was an old car engine, and a marine engine was later fitted.

Herbert Street Primitive Methodist boat
No rowlocks here - this 1920 boat had an engine.

Club members took pride in the appearance and fitting of their boats. The Naval Stores Department Boating Club was reputed to own the best equipped boat on the Tamar between 1919 and 1939, followed closely by that of the Dockyard Church. Most clubs supplied their boats with carved and painted backboards, which carried the name of the boat and the church. Ebrington St. Methodist boat was painted with a white hull and green gunwhale. The superb backboard of varnished oak was highly valued, and a member remembered 'It was a mortal sin to drop it'. The board was painted every year by a signwriter whose son was in the crew, 'in green, with lots of gold scrolls around the name *Ebrington*'.

Sherwell United Reformed Church Boating Club and their Guests
Painted backboard prominently displayed in this early 1930s picture.

Clubs also flew their own flags. The St. Jude's Guild Club flag carried the club name, Ford Methodist Boating Club had a green flag with the club name, and Morice Square Baptist Club in the 1930s flew a yellow cross on a green ground, and the letters M,S,B,C in the four quarters.

St. Budeaux Methodist Club
Members on 'anchor watch' relax beside their flag.

Some clubs rowed in a uniform. St. Boniface Boating Club crews wore berets with silver tassels, St. George's Methodist crews had white berets with red tassels, and the ladies of the Mount Gould Wesley Guild rowed their 5-oar whaler, the Perseverance, in uniform white sailor type blouses, navy skirts and white berets.

St. Boniface Church Club
Tasselled berets smartly worn in 1928.

THE BOATING CLUB MEMBERS

Most churches and chapels insisted that boating club members were church members, or at least attended the Sunday School (often in those days attended into the early twenties), a Sunday afternoon Bible class, or bodies such as the Young Men's Club or the Wesley Guild. The rules of the St. Budeaux Baptist Men's Club, as laid down in the 1919 Minute Book, declared that the Men's Boating Club was open to all male members of the Church, and all the church organisations, over the age of 15 and a half. The Senior Boating Club (mixed) at the same chapel, owned a motor boat, the *Endeavour*, and served members of the congregation, 'everyone who didn't want to row'. The membership ranged from the newly married, who wished to enjoy their boating together, rather than in single-sex clubs, to the very old.

The majority of clubs, however, were for young men, from sixteen to marriage. Clubs were formally organised, with properly constituted committees and annually elected officers, as shown on this membership card of the Royal Dockyard Sunday School Boating Club for 1926. Church affiliation was accepted by members without question, although some young men certainly changed their sectarian allegiance to obtain good boating. In 1919 Fred Cusack moved from the Anglican St. James the Great, Devonport, to Belmont Methodist Church, Stoke, which had an excellent boating club, while at the same time Mr Higgins left St. James the Great for Morice Square Baptist Boating Club.

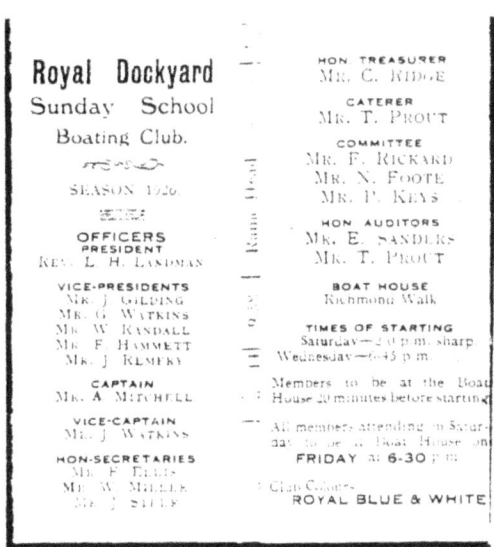

The Dockyard Church Sunday School Senior Bible Class of 1921
Formally posed and dressed in their Sunday best, and in their boat up at Weir Head during their summer camp at Calstock. The Dockyard Church boats were painted blue with a yellow streak, and were claimed to me the smartest on the river. Was the Senior Bible Class also the smartest in Devonport?

St. George's Methodist Club President
The clubs were self-governing, although most had a President, or Vice-Presidents, mature Church members who acted as the club link with the Church/Chapel management. The offices of these gentlemen were much appreciated, and Mr. Magor, the President of the St. George's Methodist Club until 1939, is seen here with the a silver presentation marking thirty years service to the Club in 1931.

Morice Square Baptist Club
A very few clubs included a mature rowing captain. The Pennycross Methodist boat was captained by the leader of the Bible Class. Morice Square Boating Club had the church organist, Theo Preston, as a rowing captain. He can be seen in the photograph sitting in the centre of the boat's stern, behind the backboard.

Information is limited, but it appears that most boating club members were the children of tradesmen, skilled Dockyard craftsmen, or members of the Royal Navy or Police: 'Father retired from the Water Police in 1930'; '[He was] the baker and gave us bags of buns for trips'; 'He owned the coal wharf [quay] at St Budeaux'. Many boating club members followed similar careers. A minority worked in shops or offices. For instance, St. Budeaux Methodist members in the 1930s were divided into two groups. 'There were two crews, as about half the club worked in offices and had Saturday afternoon free, and the other half worked in shops and had Wednesday afternoon free'. At Ford Baptist Club: 'On Wednesdays some members who worked in shops were free all the afternoon, so they took the whaler out after dinner. The Dockyard people used the gig in the evening'.

However, as was inevitable in an area when the Royal Naval Dockyard was the major employer, most boating club members were Dockyard apprentices, or craftsmen just out of their time. According to one observer, 'most of the clubs had a shipwright, a chippy and a painter, they were all apprentices'. Other past members suggested that there was some clustering of trades. For instance, at Belmont Methodist Club: 'We were mostly shipwrights and engine-fitters, not many other trades joined'. At Pennycross Methodist 'most were shipwrights by trade, though there may have been one or two boiler makers'. Ebrington Street Methodist Club in the 1930s had five painters and 'a couple of chippies'.

St. Budeaux Baptist Ladies' Club

There were at least three women's boating clubs, whose activities were more carefully supervised than those of the men's clubs. St. Budeaux Baptist Ladies' Club was formed in 1923, when the Chapel wished to provide some activity for women. Membership was restricted to Church members, and while the majority were young, with a lower age limit of sixteen, there was no upper age limit, and one lady of seventy pulled regularly in the crew. The boat *Rowena* had a male captain, Mr. Young, an ex-navy man who 'treated the girls like seamen, and could be scathing to anyone who caught a crab'. The club generated great enthusiasm, and in 1934 the Secretary, Violet Dunstan, left the chapel after her marriage to walk under the boat's oars, held aloft by a guard of honour from the crew of *Rowena*.

Belmont Methodist Church at Stoke also had a ladies' boat. Their boat, the *Hiawatha*, was financed by Mr. and Mrs. Kendall. Mr. Kendall, the Church organist, coxed the crew, chaperoned by Mrs. Kendall, the Sunday School Superintendent. The girls could invite guests, but males were limited to those staying in the crews' homes as the guests of their parents.

Belmont Ladies' Boating Club in *Hiawatha*.
Starting from the bow the ladies are Elsie Hooper, Edna and Kathleen Gunn, Kathleen Hall and Gladys Hare.

Mount Gould Wesleyan Church had a girls' crew attached to the Wesley Guild. This crew is of particular interest in that it was the only Plymouth or Devonport boating club to have a female captain. Miss Gladys Hill, Leader of the Wesley Guild and daughter of the Sunday School Superintendent, coxed the club's whaler, the *Perseverance* for several years in the 1930s. The girls' crew often rowed on excursions in company with the lads' boat from the same church.

Mount Gould Ladies' Crew
In their uniform with guests on a celebratory boating picnic at Bovisand in 1923. The authors have been assured that the bottle contained lemonade.

Although the women's clubs were strictly chaperoned, many members also boated under more liberal conditions as guests of the men's clubs.

Although most clubs were officially masculine organisations, and many young men valued and enjoyed the all-male excursions on the programme, women played an important social role in the boating clubs, since the majority of the guests introduced on 'open' excursions were female. In the Ebrington Street Methodist Boat every trip was 'open', and a past member commented that 'the lads wouldn't have come if they couldn't bring the girls'. The boating club trips provided an opportunity, unusual for the time, for groups of young men and women to meet informally, and are remembered with nostalgic affection by many very senior Plymouth and Devonport citizens. A past vice-captain of the Sherwell Congregational boat commented: 'It was a healthy and enjoyable time for young men and maidens'. At Pennycross Methodist 'the boat was a good way to meet the girls, they were always allowed to come in the boat with the lads, as mothers thought there was safety in numbers, and anyhow it was a church activity'. According to a senior member of St. Budeaux Baptist Men's Club, who remembered the first church boat, used between 1902 and 1914: 'Lads and girls of the Church formed friendships which, in quite a number of cases, culminated in marriage'. The girls, however, in that stricter age, were expected to be home by 9 pm, and one guest of the Pennycross boat remembered her last excursion with the club when the boat stuck on a Tamar mudbank on a falling tide, so that she was not home before 9.30 pm. Although in her mid-twenties she was forbidden by her parents ever to make another boating club excursion. Similar prohibitions were meted out to girls who were stuck on a sandbank with the St. Matthews boat until the early hours of the morning.

The mixed excursions certainly contributed to individual social development. '[A member] was not allowed by his mother to have girl friends, so brought his sister. He did, however, make the best of his opportunities on these trips'. The Pennycross Club, like some others, encouraged ladies to row, sharing a thwart and an oar with a member.

Pulling Together
Devonport Y.M.C.A. Senior Boating Club en-route to the Breakwater, during an Open Meeting 1921.

Individual Enterprise
Whit Monday, 1921, when the Devonport Y.M.C.A. Senior boat rowed to Jennycliffe.

A Bevy of Guests
Mount Gould Wesley Guild Men's boat, the *Rivera*, at Blagdon's Yard, River Plym, with guests, 1926.

Some churches had supervised junior boating clubs (boys only). For example, St. Budeaux Baptist Juvenile Boating Club for boys between 11 and 15 and a half was formed in 1920, and used the Men's boat for a short time before buying one of its own. The Devonport Y.M.C.A., had a junior boat before 1914, shared between the Boating Club and the Sea Scouts.

Devonport Y.M.C.A. Junior Boat *Aurora*, about 1932
With its club members (above), and (below) full of Scouts.

Roman Catholic St. Joseph's, Devonport, had a whaler which until 1923 was monopolised by the church Sea Scouts. At St. Michaels R.C., Stoke, Father Dewey ran a boys' boating club. Some of the adult club leaders became highly respected local legends. Frank Reburn ran safe boating at the Y.M.C.A. for many years, and Father Biggs electrified his St. Joseph's flock by boating in Scout Uniform, including shorts and a gold braided boating cap.

THE COST OF BOATING

Most maintenance work was carried out by members.

Herbert Street Primitive Methodist
Engine work in progress 1933.

Ford Methodist
Members at work on *Concordia*, about 1930.

However, in addition to the purchase of boats, oars, cushions, flags and picnic gear, clubs needed to pay for moorings. According to boatman Sam Webber, who supplied moorings for eight club boats at his yard at Richmond Walk in the 1930s, mooring charges were a shilling per week per boat. This covered bow and stern moorings March-September, the use of a dinghy, shed space for oars, cushions and other equipment, haul out, and winter storage, with space to fit out in the spring. St. Budeaux Baptist Men's Club paid £1 per season for moorings at Camel's Head in 1921. Some clubs managed to avoid any payment for winter storage. For instance, at Herbert Street the boat *Herbert* and the engine were stored at the back of the chapel through the winter. Also St. Budeaux Baptists started to build a new chapel in 1902, but the money ran out so that the basement was left uncompleted. For some years it served for winter storage for the church boats.

Boats were purchased, equipped, and maintained, in theory, from members' subscriptions. The Devonport Y.M.C.A. included boating as one of the activities run by the centre, but extra subscriptions were charged. In April 1909 the *Devonport Y.M.C.A. Magazine* noted that the Boating Club subscription would be 'two shillings plus the weekly fee', and expressed the hope that 'a large number of fellows will join, and that we may have a rattling good season'. In 1922 an entrance fee of one shilling and six pence, plus the weekly fee was required, and in 1934 members who paid their entrance fee before 5 May were asked for 3d., those who paid after that date 6d., with a fee of 3d. for each boat trip and a charge of 6d. for each male guest introduced. There was no charge for ladies brought as guests. St. Budeaux Baptist Men's Boating Club in 1919 paid an annual subscription of one shilling, with an additional 3d. per week in the season, while the Ladies' Club attached to the same church between 1923 and 1939 paid no annual subscription, but 2d. per boat trip covered the member and a friend. Ebrington Street Methodists also paid 3d. per week. A past member has pointed out that these subscriptions and weekly charges should be considered in the light of wages in the 1920s, a time when he was on good money, £3.10s. weekly as a journeyman, but a labourer earned only £2.10s.

Subscriptions and boat trip fees were supplemented by the profits from winter 'socials' organised by members, and stalls at church sales. Ebrington Street Methodist Chapel had a huge annual bazaar, where the Boating Club stall regularly cleared £20-30 towards boat maintenance. In one year Ebrington members organised a production of *The Pirates of Penzance* with which they toured other chapels 'and made money for the boat every time'.

The churches and chapels often gave emergency financial help to their boating clubs. That given by St. Budeaux Baptist Chapel is well documented. The Men's Boating Club rowed from 1902, but their boat rotted in storage between 1914 and 1918, and when the club was re-formed in 1919 it was estimated that a new boat and twelve oars would cost £6. The Chapel provided a loan of £6 for the initial purchase, and a member of the congregation lent a piece of land and a shed for boat maintenance. Prominent members of the congregation were also invited to 'subscribe to the funds and become honorary members'. The Boating Club Minute book in April 1919 acknowledged the help of Lieut. Sanders and the Misses Cobb, Ranbridge and Angle in the purchase of the boat. In 1921 the Church management were informed of a club financial crisis by a message from the Boating Club Committee: 'We are reluctantly compelled to forego our annual offering in view of our precarious finances and the condition of our club boats'. The problem was resolved by asking each member to pay twelve weeks boating money (three shillings) in advance, while the Chapel suggested that the Club should arrange a steamer trip for the congregation on Whit Monday, putting the profits into club funds. The Ladies' Boating Club was later encouraged to raise money for a dinghy and bathing tent by the sale of home-made sweets to the congregation after the Sunday morning services.

In addition to general boat expenses, most clubs victualled their voyages. Club teas varied in lavishness and quality. For instance, the St. Budeaux Baptist clubs provided the kettle, milk, sugar and tea, while members brought their own pasties. Stonehouse Methodist teas varied according to their current funds. When in funds they might enjoy tuff cakes, jam and cream, and sometimes even doughnuts and saffron buns. St. Levan Wesleyan Club was well known for the excellent boating teas supplied. The picnic was taken 'in a big basket from Pooley's' and usually included 'tuff cakes with jam and cream, slab cake, congress tarts', and 'sometimes the boat would call at Saltash for cockles or winkles'. Morice Square Baptists had more exotic tastes and 'always took tins of pineapple chunks. We usually remembered the tin-opener, but when it was forgotten there were ways and means.'

Herbert Street Club with Picnic Gear, May 1932

Pennycross Methodist Club expected lady guests to supply the tea, and cook the meal over a wood fire.

Ford Methodist Club
Brewed up on a Primus stove.

Dockyard Church Club
They enjoyed their picnic...

....but were then faced with the washing up.

THE EXCURSIONS

The main activity for most clubs was cruising in the Tamar and the Sound. There are some club programmes which have survived. For instance, between 3 May and 27 August 1919 the St. Jude's Guild boat made eighteen Saturday afternoon excursions, two full day trips on Bank Holidays, and rowed on seventeen Wednesday evenings. Most trips were to local beauty spots, and guests could be taken on the two Bank Holidays and 'open trips'(guest nights) on nine of the Wednesday evenings.

The Devonport Y.M.C.A Fixture List for 1935
It can be seen that in 1935 the club boated from 11 May to 4 September, visiting, like St Jude's in 1919, local beauty spots.

SATURDAY TRIPS, start 2-15 p.m.
* start 2 p.m.

Date	Destination	H.W. P.M.
May 5	Sandway	11-0
,, 12	Lopwell *	6.1
,, 19	Camp	10-8
,, 26	Weir Quay	4-41
June 2	Penlee	10-13
,, 9	St. Germans	4-00
,, 16	Yealm *	9-19
,, 23	Ince Castle F.	2-54
,, 30	Polhawn	9-15
July 7	Landulph F.	3-12
,, 14	Notter Bridge *	8-22
,, 21	Sports	12-34
,, 28	Tideford	8-14
Aug. 4	Camp	1-10
,, 11	Camp	7-22
,, 18	Bovisand	11-21
,, 25	Lopwell	7-8
,, 27	Monday. Mystery Trip	8-30

Monday and Thursday evenings are impromptu.
F. Fishing Trips.

WEDNESDAY (open) TRIPS, start 7-15 p.m.

Date	Destination	H.W. P.M.
May 9	Jennycliffe	3-32
,, 16	Millbrook	8-25
,, 23	Sandway	1-51
,, 30	Forder	7-42
June 6	Breakwater	1-53
,, 13	South Down	7-31
,, 20	Cattewater	11-57
,, 27	Antony	6-43
July 4	Kingsand	12-23
,, 11	Anderton	6 35
,, 18	Jennycliffe	10-26
,, 25	Obelisk Fields	5-54
Aug. 1	Cawsand	10-51
,, 8	Camp	4-39
,, 15	Torpoint Lawn	9-24
,, 22	Thig-a-ine	4-24
,, 29	Sandway	9-42

All Trips are liable to alteration at Committee's discretion.

There were some differences between the St. Jude's and the Y.M.C.A. programmes. Two Saturday trips for the Y.M.C.A. club were designated 'fishing trips', and, in addition to the regular Saturday and Wednesday fixtures shown on the fixture list, members could enjoy 'impromptu trips' on Monday and Thursday nights. Other clubs also used 'impromptu' excursions. For instance, St. George's Methodist Club in 1939 produced a fixture list for Saturdays from 2 May to 2 September, but had 'open' nights every Wednesday to 'impromptu' destinations.

Sunday use of the boats was normally forbidden, but there were a few exceptions. Pennycross Methodist boat sometimes took the church choir to sing in the Millbrook Chapel or delivered local preachers to Forder. Belmont lads were allowed to use the boat for weekend camps, provided they attended the service at the nearest chapel to the camp site on the Sunday morning.

Many boating clubs rowed long distances. Some landed on the Mewstone or up the Yealm, and many visited Rame and Cawsand for picnics.

Pennycross Methodist Club 1924
Enjoying an excursion to Cawsand.

Ford Methodist Club at the Breakwater
The Breakwater was a favourite destination for boating clubs. The Club are shown with primus stoves before preparing tea on the Breakwater. Credulous new crew members were frequently sent to buy vegetables from the Breakwater cabbage patch for tea.

More Fun at the Breakwater
A popular activity was climbing up into the Breakwater Cage, like this party from the Devonport Y.M.C.A., and one lad from the Kitto Settlement boat was reputed to have done a handstand on the top.

Simply Up the River
In contrast, other clubs enjoyed cruising up the River. Past members describe boating club excursions as most enjoyable social occasions. Most clubs landed to picnic, some played football, picked blackberries or other fruit, walked or bathed. Some, like these members of Herbert Street Primitive Methodist Boating Club, just relaxed in the sun.

River Rites

Some crews used boat trips to carry out special rituals, as when St. Budeaux Methodist crew in 1935 finished their picnic by staging a solemn oath never to marry (most of them did within the year). In the picture Frank Newman (with can) and Harold Ellis administer the oath to Eddy Ellis.

The Herbert Street Club Fly the Flag

The club boats could also be used to celebrate national occasions, as in this picture, but this trip and the celebration have not yet been identified and dated. Was it maybe Empire Day?

St. Budeaux Baptists
Swimming from their boat, a popular Summer activity with all the clubs.

Ford Methodists in the Swim
The boy centre back is George Pollard. Others, left to right, are Stan Espinal, R.Rickard, Arnold Baker, William Ward, Ernie Wooley, ?, Jim Fudge, Les Thomas, Sid Payne, Les Morrish, Harry Pollard and Fred Parsons.

Many clubs simply enjoyed the river and coastal scenery, the rowing, and good company.

The Senior Y.M.C.A. Boat Makes an Elegant Landing, about 1930

Herbert Street Club near Calstock
Whit Monday 1933.

Some members recalled unique excursions and happenings. St. George's Methodist boat in the early thirties had a memorable overnight trip, when they rowed to Weir Quay, waited until midnight, then went on to Calstock, left the boat ashore, and walked to Kit Hill to see the sun rise, then returned to the boat and rowed home to their mooring. The club attempted to repeat the experience the next year, when all went well as far as Weir Quay, when rain set in. The crew spent an uncomfortable night in an abandoned lime kiln, then returned home in soggy misery with 'Saltash rigs' the next day.

More happily, in 1927 St. George's Methodist boat landed at Ince Castle and were playing football when they looked up to see Lindbergh's *Spirit of St Louis* fly overhead after the first transatlantic flight.

Most clubs had favourite places and special annual trips. For example, Ford Methodist Club rowed at Midsummer by moonlight in the Sound, with floodlit bathing at the Hoe, and a midnight return to their moorings at Saltash Passage. Mount Gould Ladies enjoyed moonlight rows and picnics. St. Budeaux Baptist Ladies also gained parental leave in the mid-1930s to row in September to Landulph under the full Harvest Moon, when they landed and cooked supper, and traditionally ended the season by a second moonlight row on the Hunter's Moon in October. Landulph was a favourite destination for this crew. The ladies' boat was used in the fruit seasons to carry the crew to the cherry orchards as pickers, and on the Monday before the Church Flower Show the club always went to Landulph 'filled the boat with flowers, and brought them back to the Church'.

Summer camps became a valued aspect of boating club activities between 1920 and 1939. The Y.M.C.A. fixture list in 1935 included two camps, and the Y.M.C.A. kept tents, cooking equipment, and blankets at a site at Lopwell, Ford Methodist also used Lopwell, while St. George's Methodists camped at Weirhead in 1936. The Dockyard Church Boating Club took their equipment up river to Calstock in two boats, sometimes with the help of the Police launch as far as Saltash Bridge.

The Dockyard Church Boat Tows Equipment for their Calstock Camp 1922

St. Bartholomew's camped at Noss Mayo in 1939, and St. Boniface's Church Boating Club camped at Calstock in 1928. Ford Baptist Club camped annually at Halton Quay, where the farmer was a Church member and ex-boat club member. Most photographs of boating club camps show bell tents grouped around a central flag-pole, which flew the club flag, with the backboard of the club boat at the base of the pole.

St. Jude's Boating Club Camp up the Yealm, 1920

St. George's Methodist Boating Club Camp at Weir Head, 1936
Note the use of the club flag and the boat backboard.

Members' stories suggest that camp diet was rugged. A member of the Dockyard Church reported that at camp the lads lived on figgy duff and beef. The duff was so tough that on one occasion it was used successfully as a football. He also claimed that on one occasion, taking a short cut from the butcher's across a mudbank, he dropped the beef deep into mud, but washed it off in the river and no-one complained. He got into much more trouble later when he carried his visiting girl friend across the same mud-bank, tripped and dropped her. (She married him later in spite of it).

Many crews, like modern young people, took their music with them to camp and on excursions.

Essential Equipment for St. Boniface Boating Club in 1928
This club took a large wind-up horn gramophone with them. The Ebrington Street Club did the same, although they had trouble when records buckled in hot weather.

We Must take the Wireless!
Ford Methodist members took crystal sets with cat's whiskers (which sometimes worked). George and John Pollard are shown here trying to get results.

Most clubs sang on the pull home. A member of the Greenbank Methodist crew said they they always sang secular songs, and suggested that they sang to cover their nervousness at the prospect of taking the girls home later. Others apparently sang because they enjoyed it. In the Sherwell Congregational boat a member regularly led the singing with his ukelele, always insisting on the inclusion of 'Shine on Harvest Moon'. Ford Methodist Club claimed to have the best singing on the river, as in the late 1920s most crew members belonged to the Clarion Male Voice Choir. Most clubs sang songs of a varied nature. St. George's Methodists came home to 'Cruising Down the River', and 'Goodnight Ladies', while the Dockyard Church moored to the tune of 'When You Come to the End of a Perfect Day'. Many swept up to their moorings rowing to a hymn tune. St. Budeaux Methodists sang 'various' songs on the way home, but always finished with a couple of hymns, came up to moorings with 'The day is dying in the West', and tossed oars. Ford Methodist rowed in to 'The day thou gavest, Lord, is ended', while the St. Budeaux Baptist Ladies crew always came to moorings with 'Guide me O thou great Jehovah', and tossed oars on arrival. The Labour Party boat moored to 'The Red Flag'.

Informal racing sometimes took place between boats which met on the way home from cruises in the Sound. 'You often met half a dozen boats on the way home [from Jennicliffe] and raced for the Pool. As you rounded Batten at speed the oars could tangle and a good many were broken that way'.

For some clubs, more organised racing was as important as cruising. Some clubs raced formally in the Port of Plymouth Rowing League. This was founded and fostered by the President, Sir John Jackson, who supplied most of the prizes, and the first 'annual sports' held in 1911, attracted entries of boats from three Anglican and three Non-Conformist rowing clubs. St. George's Methodist Club crew were photographed with their trophies from this League in 1912 (Picture on back cover). Also some club boats competed in local regattas, for instance, the St. Budeaux Regatta in 1921 and the Sound Regatta in the 1930s.

St. Jude's Club Racing Crew, 1920

SAFETY

The numbers taking part in boating club excursions varied. Most clubs had rules to ensure a minimum crew for safety. Thus St. Budeaux Baptist Men's Club from 1919 insisted on a minimum crew of seven, including a member of the committee. St. Jude's had the same rule, but the Devonport Y.M.C.A. allowed five members, including one officer, to take the boat out. The personal log of John Watson, an enthusiastic member of the Dockyard Church Sunday School Boating Club, shows that in 1923 he made thirty-eight boat excursions and attended the club camp from 16-26 June. The numbers in the boat (or sometimes in two boats) as recorded by Mr. Watson, varied from seven to thirty-five, with an average crew of fourteen. The Dockyard Church, like other clubs, always tried to carry a double crew on the long hauls to the Yealm, Cawsand or the Breakwater.

Many photographs suggest that for many clubs the problem was not small crews, but an overcrowding which is disturbing to a modern observer.

St. George's Methodist Boat in 1936 at Lopwell
We are told that some additional crew members were ashore.

Devonport Y.M.C.A. Junior boat in 1914

The loading shown here was not unusual. Photographs show twenty-four adults in the St. Budeaux Baptist Ladies' 30-foot gig in 1935, while thirty-one went out with a Sherwell United Reformed Church trip in the same year. A member of Ebrington Street Club said that the 36-ft. boat sometimes took thirty-two people, so that she was loaded down to the gunwhale, and a veteran of Pennycross Methodists who happily survived many such trips commented that often in his time not only were boats overloaded, but the load was badly distributed, to allow the right boys and girls to hold hands.

The modern observer will also note that, except for a few young men with shorts, and bathing costumes for both sexes, the boating club members lacked 'leisure wear' but apparently wore their normal informal (or older) clothing. According to a St. Budeaux Baptist lady: 'We never had special clothes, we just wore a wash dress and took a cardigan'. Some girls regarded excursions as occasions to dress up, and one lady reported that she had always hoped that her parents would supply a new white hat and frock for excursions with St .John's Club, but was disappointed.

Devonport Y.M.C.A. Juniors
Even these young boys kept their caps and ties firmly on, but did not wear life jackets.

Belmont Ladies' Club
No shorts, jeans or sun-tops for these young women.

Members of boating clubs in the 1920s and 1930s had no foul weather gear, and although most excursions are remembered as blue and sunlit; 'The weather was better in those days, dear', some wet trips are vividly recalled, with strategies adopted to minimise the effects of the weather. Belmont Men's Club once met heavy rain as they rowed home down the Tamar, put the girls on the train at Bere Alston, then stripped and pulled most of the way home in their birthday suits. Ebrington Street Methodists used similar tactics, sending the ladies home by bus. St. Budeaux Ladies carried a tarpaulin for passengers, but rowers expected to get wet.

The Dockyard Boat crew expected to get wet, then to land and warm up with a game of football, or they 'warmed up' by going for a swim. At the end of June 1923, they solved the problem of one wet excursion in great style. The boat was making for Tamerton (to visit the Treacle Mines?) when rain set in. The crew diverted to Warleigh, carried passengers and tea across the mud to a disused lime kiln, lit a fire and ate strawberries and cream to dance music from their gramophone.

Although most crews included non-swimmers, no club carried or used life-jackets, none carried compass or charts: 'We wouldn't have known how to use them', and no member could re-call that any boat carried flares. There was, of course, no ship-to-shore radio or telephone communication, and there were no regular reliable local weather forecasts, except those obtainable from local knowledgable ancient mariners and boatmen. Some members used local lore. At Belmont Ladies Club : 'We used to climb to the top of Ford Hill, if you could see Kit Hill clear it would be a good day'. However, over the years senior members of the clubs built up a bank of local knowledge on the tricky tidal waters of the Tamar, Plym, and Sound, and according to the boatman Sam Webber, 'Obviously the Lord must have looked after them'.

Mr. Webber may have been right, since in spite of occasional overcrowding and lack of safety equipment, the boating clubs had a remarkably good safety record. Only two fatal accidents have been reported. In 1912 the St. Matthias Church boat capsized as it left moorings under sail, with the loss of several members. Also a member was drowned on a club outing in the Ebrington Street boat 'sometime in the 1920s' The young man was 'given a huge funeral, and the wreath from the Sunday School was in the form of an anchor'.

Some other boats had narrow escapes, but no casualties. Greenbank Methodists escaped serious damage when their boat was jammed under the jetty at Penlee Point on a rising tide. Belmont Ladies were driven ashore and partially swamped at Bovisand when a squall spang up in the Sound. St. Jude's club returned from the Yealm in fog, lost their way, and became stuck under Plymouth Pier, but both the boat and the members were undamaged. The helmsman was knocked out of the Devonport Y.M.C.A. boat by a low branch in 1923, but rescued. The Devonport Y.M.C.A. were also rescued by the police launch when a storm blew up in the Sound in the same year.

Some boats were damaged. Pennycross Methodist boat hit a rock at Mount Edgecumbe in about 1935, the damage was not serious, and the rock was thereafter known in the Club as 'Barbon's Rock' after the coxswain who found it. St. Aubyn's Church Club holed their boat when they ran onto Jennycliffe beach under full sail in 1936. Mooring to climb onto the Breakwater was somewhat hazardous. Ford Methodist Club bumped and holed their boat there, and got home by a combination of handkerchiefs stuffed into the increasing crack and constant baling. Mount Gould Ladies also holed on the Breakwater, discovered the crack when they started home, but could only get as far as Bovisand in spite of constant baling. They were fortunate to be rowing in company with the Mount Gould Men's boat, and that one of the lads was a shipwright who was able to turn the boat over on Bovisand beach to fix a temporary patch which allowed it to be rowed home.

Several boats, including Pennycross, St. Boniface and St. Budeaux Ladies, hit the underwater defence boom off Jennicliffe, but escaped serious damage. The most common mishap was stranding on a mudbank through tidal miscalculations. The Stoke Damerel Boat, coxed by the curate, took the Sunday School boys for a treat in the late 1920s, and stuck on the mud at Bere Ferrers. The small children had to be carried across the mud and cleaned up by local residents enough to be sent home by train. In many instances grounding was put right by the boys insisting on carrying the girls ashore to lighten the boat (a process much enjoyed by both groups), and the boat refloated. Other boats and crews simply had to sit on the mud until the tide came up, as in the case of Devonport Y.M.C.A. Senior Boat, who stuck on a sandbank during their summer camp at Lopwell, and stayed on the bank playing cards until 4 a.m.

Mud groundings caused considerable parental anxiety, since there was no communication with the boat, and even if a crew member could get ashore, very few families had telephones. St. Budeaux Baptist Ladies managed to contact parents after the boat stuck in the mud by means of some heroic mud-walking by a member, followed by telephone messages home via the Vicar of Landulph and the St. Budeaux Police. The Church Senior motor boat was sent up to pull them off the bank. Ironically, when the Seniors ran on the same bank off Landulph later the same season, there was no rescue for them, but most of the night had to be spent on the mud. The lack of communication also caused problems in 1928, when the St. George's Methodist crew had rowed to the Yealm. A storm came up during the afternoon and they were ordered by the Coastguards not to put to sea. Parents were so worried when the boat did not return that several fathers went to the Yealm to trace their children.

Most club members and their families were proudly honest and respectable, and there was little trouble arising from the boat trips by parties of largely unsupervised young people. However, one club disciplined some members who stole eggs at Notter Bridge during a Bank Holiday trip in May 1920. Also injudicious walking by members of another club during a visit to Barnpool resulted in an appearance in the Torpoint Magistrate's Court for trespass. According to one of the culprits the experience in court, although traumatic, paled into insignificance when compared with the later confrontation with the Chapel Minister and assembled Elders.

A Postcard from Camp
The only means of communication to home.

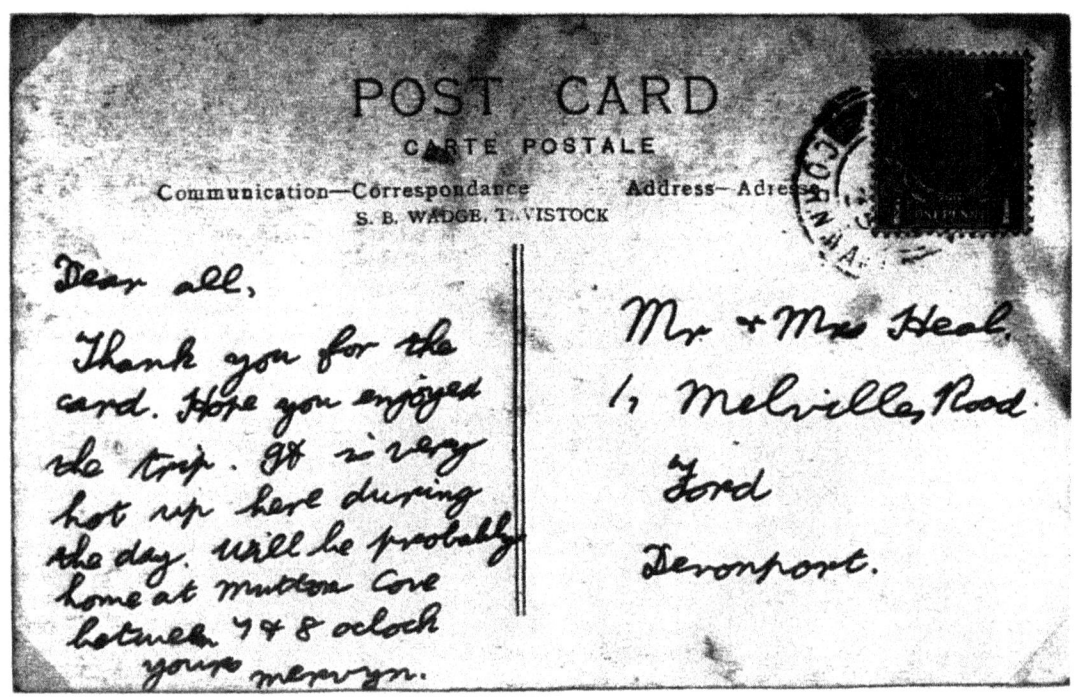

THE END OF AN ERA

The boating clubs, like other Plymouth and Devonport organisations, were affected by fluctuations in the size of the Dockyard labour force. Many past members commented that 'there was a scattering of the 1920s membership after the Geddes Axe'. Among the members of Pennycross Boating Club, 'some emigrated, one went in for teaching, two became Methodist ministers'. At Belmont, Fred Cusack and Bob Payne came out of their time, decided there was no future in the Yard and went, like many other local lads, to St. Lukes College, Exeter, to train for teaching.

At Morice Square Baptist Club, most of the members were Dockyard apprentices, who 'left Plymouth for other jobs when the Yard had bad times in the Thirties.' St George's Methodist Club was mainly composed of Dockyard apprentices in 1919, but at a reunion held in 1949 the past members included five who still worked for the Yard, including a shipwright surveyor and two senior draughtsmen, and also five teachers, one telephone engineer, three Gas Board employees, three bank clerks, two solicitors' or magistrates' clerks, one Inland Revenue official, one grocer, one master builder, and one salesman of hair restorer.

There is also some evidence that interest in club boating declined among employed young men in Plymouth and Devonport in the 1930s, a change which some past members suggest was due to the greater attraction of motor cycles. For instance, St. Aubyn's Club did not replace the boat wrecked at Jennycliffe in 1936, and when the Ebrington Street boat was dismasted and sunk at her moorings during a storm at about the same time the club closed.

Sadly, the boating clubs which lasted until 1939 did not survive the war years between 1939 and 1945, a period when boating in Plymouth was forbidden. This was partially due to the physical loss of many club boats. St. Andrew's Church boat was stored at Bere Ferrers for the duration and rotted. Ford Methodists' *Bonaventure* also rotted in storage, as did the boats from St. Budeaux Baptist Men's Club and Stoke Damerel Church. Other boats were lost through enemy action, including the Dockyard Church boats, the Pennycross boat, and the St. Bartholomew's boat, which were put into war-time storage and lost in the 1942 Blitz. The Herbert Street boat was burned with the chapel in 1942, as was the Wycliffe Wesleyan boat.

Even when the boats survived, the churches found that changed social and leisure patterns made it impossible to renew interest in club boating.

At St. Bartholomew's in 1946 the Church offered to revive the boat club, but the young people insisted on a motor boat, while their elders would only consider a rowing boat, so that the club was never restarted.

The St. Budeaux Ladies Club did enjoy a short revival. Their beloved boat *Rowena* was handed back to the Navy for war service in 1939, survived the conflict, and was returned to the church in 1945. The club re-started but never flourished and was wound up just after the Silver Jubilee celebrations in 1948.

The Post-War St. Budeaux Baptist Ladies' Boating Club.

SOURCES OF INFORMATION

PEOPLE
The following ex-members and guests of the boating clubs:

Mr. Adams, David Ayers, Rev. Alf Baker, Rev. Peter Bolt, Reg Bossom, Mrs. Bridgeman, Herbert Clarry, Nesta Cocking, Mr. Creber, Fred and Vera Cusack, John Dawson, W.Elliot, Father Foley, Mr. Gamblen Sen., Fred Gamblen, Mr. Ghillyer, J.R.Griffiths, Kathleen and Edna Gunn, Nora Hallett, Eric Hollick, Ken Hancock, Alfred and Bert Harper, Gladys Harris, Mervyn Heal, Mr. Heron, E.Higgins and Rev. Terry Higgins, Stan Hiscock, Mrs. E.Hunt, Harry Jones, Mrs. W.M.Jones, Ben Lintell, Bert Mills, Mr. Gerald Morgan, Robert Nemo, Frank Osborn, Hilda Parsons, Dennis Pittman, George Pollard, John Pollard, Mike Reburn, Wynne and Maurice Richardson, Allen Rowe, C.H.Rowe, David Salt, G.R.Sidney, Norman Sitters, Margaret Slade, Mrs. Smith, Christopher Stoneman, Violet Waldron, Tom Wales, Marshall Ware, John and Gertrude Watson, Sam Webber, boatman, Mrs H.West, Dorothy White, J.H.White, W.Whitehead, Fred Williams, Miss Gladys Woods, Kathleen Wyatt.

They told us about boating clubs attached to:

Albert Road Church, Belmont Methodist Church, Camel's Head Club, Catholic Young Men's Society, Devonport Methodist Central Hall, Devonport Y.M.C.A., Dockyard Church Sunday School, Ebenezer Baptist Chapel, Ebrington Street Methodist Church, Ebrington Street Wesleyan Chapel, Emmanuel Church, Ford Baptist Chapel, Ford Methodist Church, Gloucester Street Methodist Church, Greenbank Methodist Church, Haddington Road Chapel, Herbert Street Primitive Methodist Church, Keyham Methodist Church, King Street Wesley Methodist Church, Kitto Settlement, Morice Square Baptist Chapel, Mount Gould Wesley Guild, Mutley Baptist Chapel, Naval Stores Department, Pembroke Street Pub, Pennycross Methodist Church, Plymouth Police, Royal Albert Bridge Inn, St. Andrews Church (Plymouth), St. Aubyn's Church, St. Bartholomew's Church (Higher Stoke), St. Boniface Church (St. Budeaux), St. Budeaux Baptist Chapel, St. Budeaux Methodist Church, St. Budeaux Y.M.C.A., St.Chad's Church, St.George's Church (Devonport) (Anglican), St. George's Road Methodist Church, St.James the Great Church (Devonport), St. John's Church (Devonport), St. Joseph's Church (Devonport) (R.C.), St. Jude's Church, St. Levan's Wesleyan Church, St. Mark's Church, St. Mary's Church (Devonport), St. Matthias Church, St. Michael's (Stoke) (R.C.), St. Nicholas & Faith Church (Saltash), St. Stephen's Church (Devonport), Saltash Baptist Church, Sherwell Congregational (later United Reformed) Church, Stoke Damerel Church, Stonehouse Boys' Club, Stonehouse Wesleyan Church, Sutton Harbour Labour Party, Virginia House, Wycliffe Methodist Church.

DOCUMENTS
Devonport Y.M.C.A. *Handbook* (1915).
Devonport Y.M.C.A. Magazine 3 (1909).
Devonport Y.M.C.A. Magazine *Progress* 15 (1922).
Devonport Y.M.C.A. Boating Club Fixture Card, 1934.
St. Budeaux Baptist (Men's) Boating Club, Minute Book, 1919-22.
St. George's Methodist, Fixture card,1939.
St. George's Methodist Club, programme of reunion held at Stoke, 28 Dec. 1949.
St. Jude's Guild Rowing Club Fixture List, 1919.
John Watson, Dockyard Church Boating Club, personal Boating Club Log for 1923.
Fred Cusack 'Clinker Built Pleasure" in *Western Morning News* 9 February 1983.

Arthur L. Clamp – the man behind the books

Arthur Leslie Clamp was a man of boundless energy with a passion for helping others, particularly through his love of history. A printer by trade, he started his career in a printing company before moving his family from Exeter to Plymouth to teach at the Plymouth College of Art and Design, where he eventually became the Head of the Printing Department.

A Devoted Family Man

Arthur with his five children.

Despite his love of teaching, Arthur prioritised his family, always making it home by 5:30pm for tea. He and his wife, Rosemary, raised five children: Susan, Angela, Elizabeth, David, and Steven. Arthur would often combine his love of family and history by taking his children on Sunday walks, encouraging them to appreciate historical monuments by taking photos or making crayon rubbings of gravestones for his books. The family home at 203 Elburton Road was a hub of activity, with a large garden, featuring a two-storey fort and a makeshift swimming pool.

A Lifelong Learner and Adventurer

Arthur's thirst for knowledge extended beyond history to a deep curiosity about the world. He was passionate about exploring different cultures, traditions, and cuisines, often taking advantage of his long summer holidays as a teacher to travel to places like India, Russia, South America, the middle east and the USA, sometimes bringing one of his children along. This adventurous spirit even influenced his home life, as seen by the short-lived family tradition of steam-cooking vegetables after a trip to Iceland.

History is a prominent feature of family days out

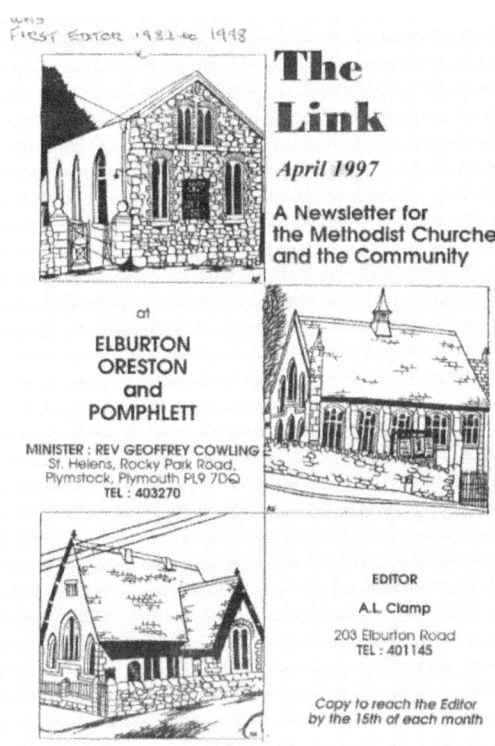

Community and Philanthropic Spirit

His commitment to serving others was evident in his long-standing involvement with the Elburton Methodist Church. He was the Sunday School Superintendent for over 15 years and served as the editor of the wider church's monthly newsletter, "The Link," for a similar duration. After Rosemary's very sad passing, Arthur later remarried and, following a chance encounter with a professor from India, established a connection with a missionary school in Chennai. Together with his new wife, Christine, he co-founded a "Sponsor a Child's Education" program that continues to this day.

Pictured left – The cover of 'The Link' complete with hand drawn sketches of each church by Angela
Below right – Arthur Clamp promoting his latest book
Below left – Arthur at home with his first wife, Rosemary
Below centre – Arthur on holiday with his second wife, Christine

A Legacy of Learning and Positivity

Arthur's greatest passion was history, which he brought to life through tireless research, documentation, and the many books he authored. He was driven by a need to "never be stuck in a rut," constantly seeking new experiences, meeting new people, and expanding his knowledge. With a positive attitude and a great sense of humour, he was always ready to help others, leaving a lasting impact on his family and community. His children, Susan, Angela, Elizabeth, David, and Steven, remember him with love and gratitude.

David Clamp, 2025

A Legacy of Local History

Below is the story of how Arthur L Clamp began writing books, in his own words, drafted shortly before he passed away in 2001. I have only made minor alterations to this text, correcting grammatical errors that he did not survive to correct himself. When I first discovered this text, I was shocked to see my name mentioned. It seems that, unbeknownst to me, I shared my first PC with him. I suspect he used it during the day when I was at school, although I do have one memory of sitting with him and showing him how it worked. It has been a pleasure to pick up where he left off and see his books republished and redistributed, and to know that I was part of the story, even back then. It was also fascinating to discover that his pricing structure matches the way I have tried to price the books, with a third going to local sellers and the rest covering printing costs with a little left over for my expenses.

I am his eldest grandson, and it is a privilege to curate his legacy, which we are calling 'The Clamp Collection'. The very last line of the text originally reads "The following pages list all the titles." Sadly, that page is missing and we have no record of all the books he published and knowing that some of those were researched by other authors makes the process of finding them even harder. I look forward to one day completing the collection and seeing them all available again. And maybe, one day, I'll even start writing my own to add to the series. For now, here is his story in his own words.

Steven Gibson, 2025

Writing and Publishing Booklets on Local Topics and Areas

I started this interest in either 1968 or 1969 when living in Woodford. I had by these dates established the Department of Printing and I think I must have been looking for something different to do. The first titles were of A5 size proofed from type set at Clarke, Doble and Brendon, Ltd., Plymouth printers, and then made up into pages and printed at Sawtell and Neilson, Ltd., Totnes.

Then began a slow process of getting them out to shops, etc. which proved to be more time consuming and difficult than actually researching, writing and getting the books into print. However, I persisted and opened a business account with Barclays Bank on the Broadway. I was advised to give it a title so I called it "Westway Publications". There came along another problem, one of storage of paper and finished books which was solved when the family moved to Elburton in 1970.

I changed the printer to Penwell, Ltd., Callington, Cornwall, as he was then just setting up himself and his prices seemed very reasonable. I did not get any of the printers to make up the complete books. I hand folded the flat printed sheets, stitched the books on a small manual table stitcher and trimmed them in a small hand turned guillotine which I bought from someone in Penzance for £40. It was brought up in a van.

The trouble and time going to and fro to Callington was too much so I transferred the printing to PDS Printers, Prince Rock, Plymouth, and I have been with them ever since. Now they are at Plympton which is easy to reach and they fold the flat sheets which was turning out to be a long chore which only saved a small part of the printing costs.

All my first titles were written by myself. I took the photographs and developed them in the loft of the house, the type was set by now on a computer situated in the house at Elburton from which I had collected photographic lengths of text to cut up and law down as pages.

At some point I decided that I would do my own film processing of lith film so I bought a large second hand process camera from Kingsbridge and learnt through trial and error to make line negatives of the text and halftone negatives of the illustrations which proved more difficult than I anticipated. The main problem was trying to keep the developer in the large dish at the correct temperature as any change would affect the developing time. I replaced this old camera with a brand new one bought from Croydon, Surrey, costing £900. This has turned out to be a great asset cutting out an expensive part of the printer's costs and one crucial aspect of the work which I could control.

By the middle 1970s there were many outlets I had contacted in Plymouth, up to Dartmoor, Exeter, around to Torbay, Totnes, Dartmouth and the South Hams. The market for local books was much greater than I had first thought and through getting to know many local people undertaking research themselves had the chance to help and make up books for other people who had in most instances, got together a collection of photographs with some text in a rather muddled way. Through my experience in print I was able to shape up their work and get it into print and in every case I had to pay the printer and let the person have the royalties. In the majority of titles produced in this manner this was another way of producing titles and it did give some profit to my work. However, I must say that in a few cases I lost out by either the other person getting the numbers wrong, not returning any monies from stock I delivered or they thought that more of their books should have been sold.

The print run was usually 1,000 copies and from time to time I have had reprints of 250 copies. It took about ten years to clear the first print run so I always had large stocks in the garage, workshop, etc. The numbers sold during the early years was about 7,000 copies a year increasing to around 9,000 copies and for the whole of the enterprise about 500,000 have been sold. The booklets have become part of the local scene and many people collect them, shops regularly order copies and I go around certain areas month by month restocking or replacing titles as necessary.

During the past year or so I have started setting the text on a Packard Bell PC, something which I should have done some years back. I share it with Steven Gibson, my grandson. There appears to be no end to the market for local books, but I could not earn a regular income because of the long time it takes to sell stock.

However, now exceeding 100 titles made up mainly of A4 twenty-four page booklets, some folded guides, with selling prices set with a third going to the shop which is the trade custom, the original idea has been quite successful and could go on for ever.

Apart from monetary benefits, however spasmodically these might be, I have learnt a lot myself, met many interesting people and have become part of the local scene with requests to give talks and to advise people about getting into print.

Arthur L Clamp, 2001

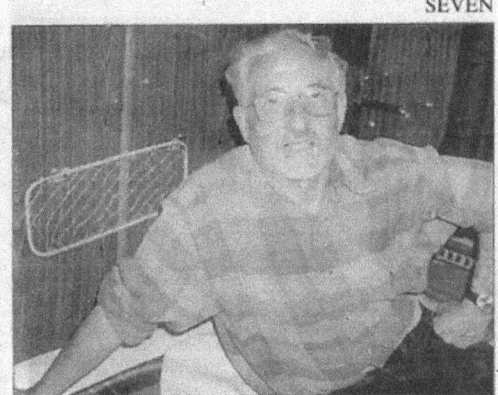

This newspaper article, published by the Evening Herald on 17th August 2001, forms a good record of his life. Just as he encourages us to learn more about local history, we encourage you to learn a little about him. For that reason, we have included these pages at the back of all the most recently republished books, in honour of his memory and recognition of his contribution to the community.

www.ingramcontent.com/pod-product-compliance
Lightning Source LLC
Chambersburg PA
CBHW061404070526
44584CB00031B/4159